Too Small

17 NOV 2020

First published by
Evans Brothers Limited
2A Portman Mansions
Chiltern St
London WIU 6NR

Reprinted 2006

British Library Cataloguing in Publication Data

Woodward, Kay
      Too small. - (Zig zags)
      1. Children's stories - Pictorial works
      I. Title
      823.9'2 [J]

ISBN 0 237 52777 4

13-digit ISBN (from I January 2007) 9780237527778

Printed in China by WKT Company Limited

Series Editor: Nick Turpin
Design: Robert Walster
Production: Jenny Mulvanny
Series Consultant: Gill Matthews

ZIG ZAG

Too Small

by Kay Woodward
illustrated by Deborah van de Leijgraaf

Evans

Max is small.
His big brother Bob is tall.

Bob has lots of tall
friends.

"You can't play with us,
Max," they say.
"You're too small."

Bob and his friends play basketball.

But Max is too small.

Bob and his friends ride bikes.
But Max is too small.

Bob and his friends play
swing ball.

But Max is too small.

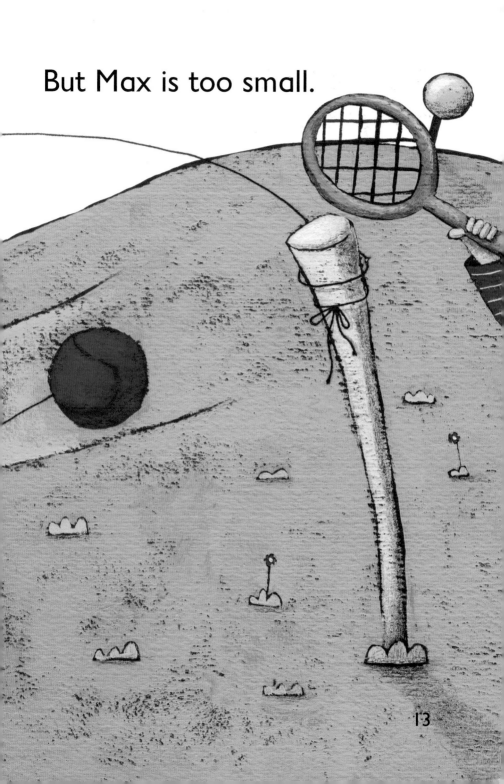

Bob and his friends play leapfrog.

Max is much, much too small.

"I want to play!" shouts Max.

No one listens.

Max is fed up.
He's too small for
everything.

Splish-splash. It starts to rain.

21

"What shall we play?"
asks Bob.

Max has an idea.

"Let's play hide and seek," he says.

24

Bob counts to ten.

Time to hide!

They squeeze. They squish.
They squash.

But they're too big!

Max isn't too big … and he isn't too small.

He's just right.

Max has the best hiding place of all!

Why not try reading another ZigZag book?

Dinosaur Planet   ISBN 0 237 52793 6
by David Orme and Fabiano Fiorin

Tall Tilly   ISBN 0 237 52794 4
by Jillian Powell and Tim Archbold

Batty Betty's Spells   ISBN 0 237 52795 2
by Hilary Robinson and Belinda Worsley

The Thirsty Moose   ISBN 0 237 52792 8
by David Orme and Mike Gordon

The Clumsy Cow   ISBN 0 237 52790 1
by Julia Moffatt and Lisa Williams

Open Wide!   ISBN 0 237 52791 X
by Julia Moffatt and Anni Axworthy

Too Small   ISBN 0 237 52777 4
by Kay Woodward and Deborah van de Leijgraaf

I Wish I Was An Alien   ISBN 0 237 52776 6
by Vivian French and Lisa Williams

The Disappearing Cheese   ISBN 0 237 52775 8
by Paul Harrison and Ruth Rivers

Terry the Flying Turtle   ISBN 0 237 52774 X
by Anna Wilson and Mike Gordon

Pet To School Day   ISBN 0 237 52773 1
by Hilary Robinson and Tim Archbold

The Cat in the Coat   ISBN 0 237 52772 3
by Vivian French and Alison Bartlett